MW01195027

Bloomsbury USA

An imprint of Bloomsbury Publishing Plc

1385 Broadway   50 Bedford Square
New York   London
NY 10018   WC1B 3DP
USA   UK

www.bloomsbury.com

First published 2016

ISBN: HB: 978-1-63286-442-0

Library of Congress Cataloging-in-Publication Data is available.

2 4 6 8 10 9 7 5 3 1

Designed and typeset by Wooden Books Ltd, Glastonbury, UK

Printed in the U.S.A. by Worzalla, Stevens Point, Wisconsin

To find out more about our authors and books visit
www.bloomsbury.com. Here you will find extracts, author interviews,
details of forthcoming events, and the option to sign up for our newsletters.

Bloomsbury books may be purchased for business or promotional use.
For information on bulk purchases please contact Macmillan Corporate and
Premium Sales Department at specialmarkets@macmillan.com.

PROVERBS

THE WISDOM OF THE WORLD

Alice O'Neill

BLOOMSBURY

NEW YORK · LONDON · OXFORD · NEW DELHI · SYDNEY

To Hector, thanks for all your help.

With sincere thanks to the staff at the Warburg Institute,
in London, for access to their astonishing picture library.

Various books and web resources have been invaluable aids in collecting and organizing
the proverbs for this little book. If you want more then I recommend: The Routledge
Book of World Proverbs, *edited by Jon R. Stone,* The Prentice-Hall
Encyclopedia of World Proverbs, *edited by Wolfgang Mieder,* The Oxford
Dictionary of Proverbs, *edited by Jennifer Speake & John Simpson, and* The
Penguin Dictionary of Proverbs, *edited by Rosalind Fergusson and Jonathan Law.*

Above: Engraving by Pieter van der Heyden [ca. 1530-1572] of a 1558
drawing of by Pieter Bruegel the Elder, showing a senile or demented
Everyman searching for who knows what in all manner of places.

CONTENTS

Introduction	1
Wisdom and Idiots	4
Advice and Ignorance	6
Substance and Appearance	8
Past, Present, and Future	10
Thought and Action	12
Friends and Enemies	14
Fight and Flight	16
Success and Failure	18
Richer and Poorer	20
Beauty and the Beast	22
Love and Lament	24
Married and Single	26
Children and Parents	28
Honor and Shame	30
Work and Play	32
Careful and Carefree	34
Excess and Deficiency	36
Lucky and Hapless	38
Hope and Despair	40
Change and Stasis	42
Power and Humility	44
True and False	46
Strong and Weak	48
Kind and Selfish	50
Young and Old	52
Health and Sickness	54
Life and Death	56
Country Codes	58

INTRODUCTION

All over the world you'll find that people pepper their speech with proverbs. These sayings reveal fascinating aspects of the common sense, morals, humor, wisdom, and history of their culture, and are vital when there is no written means of transmitting ideas and insights from one generation to the next. Proverbs are inevitably memorable, they are memes which have evolved and survived. They communicate concepts, and their use must be as old as language itself, indeed it has been said that the best way to learn a language is to learn its proverbs.

Little verbal games are much used in many proverbs: alliteration (*Forgive and forget*), parallelism (*Nothing ventured, nothing gained*), rhyme (*When the cat is away, the mice will play*) and ellipsis (*Once bitten, twice shy*). Other tricks include repeated vowels (assonance), such as this Ethiopian example: *Kan mana baala, a'laa gaala* ('A leaf at home, but a camel elsewhere'). Proverbs also frequently employ metaphor (*the squeaky wheels gets the grease*) and hyperbole (*All is fair in love and war*), as well as paradox (*For peace there must first be war*) and personification (*Hunger is the best cook*) to make their points.

A proverb's frequent purpose is to make people pause for a moment and reflect. In Gaelic-speaking Ireland, for example, a fight caused by a bad comment might be stopped with *It's often that a man's mouth broke his nose*. The listener is thus made to reflect on the absurdity of the situation, for how can a soft mouth break a hard nose?

The word 'proverb' may be defined as a short sentence or phrase that conveys a nugget of common sense, a summary of practical experience or a rule of conduct. Several other words have similar meanings, for example, 'saying', 'aphorism', 'adage', 'maxim' or 'saw'. Paremiologists (academics who study proverbs) try to draw precise boundaries between these various terms, although in reality it can be difficult to tell them apart. They would define a maxim as a statement of general principle such as *You're either part of the solution or you're part of the problem*, while an aphorism has a moral or philosophical tone, such as *Maladies are cured by nature, not remedies*. Furthermore, an adage is described as an aphorism that has passed into general use, while another term, an apophthegm, is used for particularly cynically-worded sayings such as *You could cut a better man out of a hedge*.

As proverbs can employ all of these forms, they have a delightful fluidity. The best evidence we have for their antiquity is that surviving stone-age hunter-gatherer cultures such as those of the San in South Africa or the Australian aborigines use them in multitudes. Indeed, the earliest surviving book is a collection of sayings or proverbs written down in Egypt around the 25th century BC called *The Maxims of Ptahhotep*. This book covers a wide range of topics from table manners to beauty hints and ways of cultivating self-control, and the Egyptians produced many more including *The Instructions of Amememope*, circa 1300-1075 BC, which were an important source for the biblical *Book of Proverbs*. Ancient Sanskrit texts are also full of proverbs, and there are vast numbers of Chinese proverbs, including many attributed to the great fifth century BC philosopher Confucius. Indeed many of the best literary lines from Homer onwards have since become proverbs, and virtually all writers either used existing proverbs or gave the language new ones. Shakespeare gave more proverbs to the English than anyone else and often used John Heywood's *Dialogue Conteinyng The Number In Effect Of All The Prouerbes In The Englishe Tongue* of 1546 as a source, lifting from it such lines as *All's well that ends well*.

The use of rhetorical language, paradoxical statements, and purported logic in proverbs adds to their appeal, and helps them transmit their cultural insights; and the ambiguity inherent in so many is useful too, particularly for voicing sensitive opinions, such as political dissent. In Tsarist Russia people could thus express their contempt with such ironies as *When the Tsar spits into the soup dish, it bursts with pride*, but, inevitably, proverbs were also manipulated by people in power, including the Soviets, who tried to create politically correct ones such as *Good harvests come only from collective farms*. The impact of modernisation is always much celebrated, as in a recent offering from Haiti which declares that *A microwaved fish doesn't fear the lightning*.

Apart from the Egyptian examples, the earliest recorded proverbs are found in Sumerian and Akkadian collections, including one of 1800 BC which declares that *If a she-dog is too hasty it gives birth to blind puppies*. The popularity and longevity of proverbs is such that this one now turns up from Ethiopia to Holland to Afghanistan, and was also used by Erasmus in the 16th century. Indeed, all levels of belief are enshrined in proverbs, from Native American observations about how we should thank food before we eat it to the thousands found in the sacred texts of all major religions. Novelists and film-makers depend on them, and advertising gives them new outlets, from Volkswagen's *A pfennig saved is a pfennig earned* to Godiva Chocolatier's *Not only absence makes the heart grow fonder*.

These dollops of fun or good sense create such delightful verbal images that they color every conversation, and roll so easily off the tongue that it would be impossible to live without them.

WISDOM AND IDIOTS
learning the way

WISDOM: Although *Knowledge is not wisdom* [EGY], *Knowledge is harmony* [EGY], and if you *Know yourself you will know the Gods* [EGY] for *Knowing others is wisdom; knowing yourself is Enlightenment* [CHI]. Actually, *Knowledge is like water for the land* [KYR], therefore *Learn from the mistakes of others, so you don't have to make them yourself* [ENG], for it's *Better to know too much than too little* [NOR]. *Wisdom begins in wonder* [GRE] but *Wisdom only comes when you stop looking for it* [HOPI], and since *Knowledge takes up no space* [SPA] and *Learning is a treasure no thief can steal* [IND], why not *Open a school, close a prison* [FRA], for when you *Educate a woman, you educate a population* [BURU]. *To know all is to forgive all* [FRA], so *Leave half of what you know in your head* [AFR AME], and be aware that *Still waters run deep* [ROM], for *He who knows does not speak, while he who speaks does not know* [GRE]. Of course, *Not knowing is Buddha* [JAP].

4

COMMON SENSE: They say *To attain knowledge, add things every day; To attain wisdom, remove things every day* [CHI]. And since *All sense is not kept under the same roof* [NOR], *Even if you know a thousand things, always ask a man who knows something* [TUR], indeed *Seek education even if it means travelling to China* [ARAB]; but go carefully, for *In the desert of life the wise man travels in a caravan, the fool by himself* [ARAB]. It's true that *To get lost is to learn the way* [AFR], but *If you are on the road to nowhere, change the road* [ASH], and don't give up, for *Wisdom rides on the ruins of folly* [DAN] and *A disaster teaches more than a thousand warnings* [TUR]. *A wise man drinks little and believes less* [BAS] because *Wisdom is the lifelong attempt to acquire it* [AME], indeed *Only when a tree has grown can you tie your horse to it* [AFR JABO]. Always remember, *Everything is relative* [RUS], so *Everyone likes justice in another's house, none in their own* [ITA], and never forget, *Our first teacher is our heart* [NAT AME].

IDIOTS: Beware wise-looking men, as *Brains are not found in the beard* [IND], and know that *All seems the same to someone who knows nothing* [EGY], just as *In the unknown village the chickens have teeth* [IVO]. Sadly, *A fool grows without rain* [HEB] and *There is no royal road to learning* [TUR], which is why so often *The ignorant are the enemies of wisdom* [ENG]. Remember, *A person who knows little repeats it often* [BER], so *Fear a man who only knows one book* [FRA], indeed *Fear an ignorant man more than a lion* [KUR]. Listen, *A fool is known by his laugh* [GER], and *Every fool wants to give advice* [ITA], but *Try with all your might you'll not get milk from a bull* [UKR], and *A dog is no help in a smithy* [TUR], so *Only an idiot looks for a calf under an ox* [TUR]. It's *Better to leave those in error who love error* [EGY], for *By the time an idiot learns the game the players have dispersed* [ARAB], indeed *The dogs bark, the caravan passes on* [TUR]. Remember, *Even a broken clock is right twice a day* [ENG], and *Even the stupidest person seems wise if he keeps his mouth shut* [FIN], which is why *A wise man sits over the hole in his own carpet* [PER].

Advice and Ignorance
the truth can hurt

GIVING ADVICE: *There's no price for good advice* [SPA], which is why *One word to the wise is enough* [GRE], and *He that speaks sows, whereas He that hears reaps* [TUR]. *Leading by example is better than giving advice* [ARAB], so it's often best to *Say little about what you know and nothing about what you don't* [BAS], for *No matter how much care is taken, someone will be misled* [BURM]. *For many the truth hurts* [BAS], as *Good medicine is bitter to the tongue; good advice is harsh to the ear* [KOR], which is why *If you advise a bear you deserve your fate* [TUR], and *Many people use a stick for a nobody and a hint for a nobleman* [AFG]. A fool may say *Do as I say, not as I do!* [ENG] but *Even a fool can give ideas to a wise man* [AFR]. And remember, *Never give advice in a crowd* [ARAB].

HEEDING ADVICE: *He asks advice in vain who does not heed it* [FRA], so ask for what you want: *Don't offer me advice; give me money* [SPA]. *Forewarned is forearmed* [ENG] they say, so *Learn from new books and old teachers* [KUR], and if you can't read then *Experience will show you, while a master points the way* [EGY]. Remember, *It's shameful never to ask* [TUR] and *It's better to ask twice than lose your way once* [DAN], as *He who seeks advice seldom errs* [PHL]. Many a young prince is told that *Listening to good advice is the way to wealth* [PER], for *A king with good counsellors has a peaceful reign* [ASH]. Often, because *Deep calls to deep* [ITA], *One piece of good advice is better than a bagful* [DAN], and *Crafty advice often comes from a fool* [IRI]. Bear in mind that *Another person's counsel is no command* [ITA], and that you must *Examine the advice, not who gives it* [ARAB]. Remember, *If you ask a lazy person to work he will only give you advice* [TUR], but if you're lucky, you'll find *The best advice is on your pillow* [DAN] and *The best word is left unsaid* [SPA], for *All that is known is not told* [EGY].

IGNORING ADVICE: Only a bad child will not take advice [AFR], for *There's none so deaf as those who won't hear* [ITA], and *There's none so blind as those who won't see* [ENG], yet *No enemy is worse than bad advice* [GRE] because *If the blind lead the blind, both will fall into the ditch* [BIB], particularly as *Advice most needed is least heeded* [ENG]. Of course, *The person on shore is always the champion swimmer* [EGY] and *Many will show you the way after the cartwheel breaks* [TUR]. Remember, *There is no right way to a wrong thing* [TUR], and *Advice after mischief is like medicine after death* [DAN], so bear in mind that *Wise men don't need advice and Fools won't take it* [AME], so why not *Go to the square and ask advice, then go home and do what you like* [ITA].

SUBSTANCE AND APPEARANCE
books and their covers

SUBSTANCE: Things are what they are, *It is what it is* [JAP], for instance *However long a log lies in the water it never becomes a crocodile* [MALI], and *You don't gather grapes from thorns, or figs from thistles* [PER]. *Nature abhors a vacuum* [ROM], thus *The pebble comes from the mountain* [ARAB], and *Each bay has its own wind* [FIJI]. *In nature there's no such thing as a lawn* [ALB]; even if you try to *Drive out nature with a pitchfork, she'll keep coming back* [ENG]. Indeed, *Nature follows its course and a cat the mouse* [GRE], so *Cats don't catch mice to please God* [AFG]. *Human nature is the same the world over* [AME], just as *The name given to a child becomes natural to it* [AFR YORUBA]. Perhaps because of this *Sometimes a person is nothing, and some aren't even that* [FIN], so never forget, *There's a prawn under every rock* [THAI], and *To him who watches, everything reveals itself* [ITA].

APPEARANCE: It is widely held that *As is the garden, so is the gardener* [HEB], just as *There is no smoke without fire* [ITA], indeed *What you see is what you get* [ENG], so maybe *Clothes make the man* [GRE]. In most cases *Joining tail to trunk reveals the elephant* [IND], in the same way that *The background needs the foreground* [MON], and *Every hill has its valley* [ITA]. So *Appear always what you are and a little less* [GRE], for *In a flat country a hillock is a mountain* [KUR]. And *Don't judge a man until you have walked a mile in his shoes* [KUR], as *It takes all sorts to make the world* [ENG], and *All shoes are not made in the same batch* [NOR], indeed *Different ponds have different fish* [INDO]. Remember, *Appearances are deceitful* [ENG], and *Looks are nothing - behavior is all* [IND], and since the *Eyes are the window of the soul* [ROM], *What the eye doesn't see the heart doesn't grieve* [ROM].

DISGUISES: *Never judge a book by its cover* [ENG], for *A cowl does not make a monk* [SPA] and *Pretty clothes and fine faces don't make good people* [CONG], indeed

A fair skin often covers a crooked mind [DAN]. Perhaps Clothes do not make the man [ENG] after all, as Black souls wear white shirts [UKR], while A clever hawk hides its claws [JAP], and all too often Under the sheikh's turban there is a monkey [EGY]. Water can deceive the diver [EGY] as well, so don't be a fool: Don't think there are no crocodiles if the water is still [MALAY], and remember, A sweet potato doesn't advertise that he's tasty [MAORI], just as The tree with most leaves doesn't always have juicy fruit [BRA]. It goes without saying that Not all white liquids are milk [IND], just as Not all black objects are coal [BAS], and A sandal is not a shoe [AFG]. So look deeper, and see that The grey mare may be the better horse [ENG] despite the fact that A bad horse will eat as much as a good one [DAN], and watch out, There are often glowing embers under cold ashes [DAN]. Remember, Eat what you like but dress as others do [ARAB]: Goodness whispers, but evil shouts [BAL].

PAST, PRESENT AND FUTURE
any time will do

PAST: We all know how *Time flies* [ROM], how it is *Here today and gone tomorrow* [ENG], how *No hand can catch time* [IND]. Indeed, *Time is precious* [ENG], *Time is money* [AME], though all too often *We want time badly, then use it badly* [AME]. For example, *Don't let yesterday take up too much of today* [NAT AME], and *Don't cry over spilt milk* [ENG], for *There are no birds in last year's nest* [ENG]. In general, *Hindsight is clearer than foresight* [ENG], so remember, *Four things do not return: spoken words, flighted arrows, past life, and lost opportunities* [ARAB]; indeed, *Even a god can't change the past* [GRE], for *A lost sheep can be recovered, but not lost time* [BAS]. Despite this, *No matter how hard the past, you can always begin again* [ZEN]; and when you do, watch out, *History repeats itself* [ENG], which is why so often *Things present are judged by things past* [IND], and *Today is the scholar of yesterday* [ROM].

PRESENT: *The early bird catches the worm* [ENG], for so often in life it's *First come first served* [FRA] and *If you get to the river early you drink the cleanest water* [AFR]. Otherwise, you can tell yourself *Better late than never* [ENG], for *Everything has its proper time, Even manuring cabbages* [GRE]. Indeed, there's *A time for adversity, a time for prosperity* [TAM], and *There's a first time for everything* [ENG]—even *The longest journey starts with a single step* [CHI]. Aim to *Experience each moment to its fullest* [ZEN], for *There's no time like now* [ENG], and despite the fact that *Time and tide wait for no man* [ENG] and *The tide must be taken when it comes* [ENG], don't forget to *Give time time* [ITA], to *Suit yourself to the times* [GER], and remember that *Time brings roses* [ENG]. Indeed, *Those who are happy do not observe the passing of time* [CHI], and *One today is worth two tomorrows* [ENG].

FUTURE: *Worrying about the future ruins the present* [ENG], so relax, *Tomorrow is another day* [ENG], and *Tomorrow's winds will blow tomorrow* [JAP], so *Let us think of tomorrow when tomorrow comes* [PER], though *Tomorrow never comes* [AME]. In the end *Time heals all* [ENG], for *Everything has an end* [UZB] and *Things will work out* [AME], *All in good time* [ENG]. Just remember *The past is the future of the present* [JAP]; indeed, *We are only visitors to this time and place* [AB AUS], *With a sponge to wipe away the past, a rose to sweeten the present and a kiss to greet the future* [ARAB], for *Flowers bloom, flowers fall* [CHI].

11

THOUGHT AND ACTION
practice and preaching

THINKING: *Everyone who succeeds must first dream* [MANCOPA], so remember that *Your head is not just there for a hat* [UKR], and that *If you fail to plan, you plan to fail* [AME]. At the very least, *Don't go out of your depth before you can swim* [ENG], because *If you know the road you can ride full trot* [ITA], but if you don't then *Ask those coming back for the best way forward* [CHI]. *A person in a hurry arrives late* [GEOR] whereas *Slow and steady wins the race* [ENG], so *First catch your hare* [ENG], because once you know how, *To know and to act are the same* [JAP]. That's why *Practice makes perfect* [ENG] and *Repetition is the mother of memory* [AME], and also why *A pleasant thought never comes too soon* [DAN]. So be aware that *A tree only moves if there's wind* [AFG], and *A watched pot never boils* [ENG], which is why you *Don't call a dog with a whip in your hand* [AFR] and *A big goat does not sneeze without a reason* [MALAW].

DECIDING: Some say that *The world is conquered with words, not swords* [GEOR], though this is *Easier said than done* [EUR], for *Fine words don't put porridge in the pot* [BOT]. Of course, *Thought is free* [ENG], and *Anything that releases you from a dilemma is useful* [AFR FULANI] but remember that *It's easier to think than to act* [GER], and *You don't get anywhere by running in your mind* [FIN]. Nevertheless, the mind is powerful, *Work doesn't kill, but worry does* [AFR], and *If you think something impossible, it will be* [TUR], just as *If the heart is unwilling it will make a thousand excuses* [INDO]. That's why *Where there's a will there's a way* [ENG], and *What isn't can yet be done* [GER] for *You already have all you need to become great* [NAT AME]. Above all, always try to *Do unto others as you would have them do unto you* [BIB], and *Never say never* [ENG]. Of course, *Smooth hands love the labour of others* [RUS], and the coward will

always say "When in doubt, don't" [ITA], for No choice is also a choice [HEB], but even if The spirit is willing but the flesh is weak [ENG], generally, Elbow grease is the best polish [ENG].

ACTION: A rocky field demands a pickaxe not a prayer [NAT AME], so Never put off for tomorrow what you can do today [ENG], for Even if the eyes fear, the hands will do the work [RUS]. Of course, Least said soonest mended [ENG], and Actions speak louder than words [ENG], so it's mostly Better to have less thunder in the mouth and more lightning in the hand [NAT AME], for when you Grasp a nettle like a lad of mettle, as soft as silk it will remain [ENG]. In the same spirit, Put your best foot forward [ENG], aim to Be the master of your will and the slave of your conscience [HEB], and If your destiny doesn't fit, then fit yourself to your destiny [ARAB]. All Actions have reactions [KOR], so Practice what you preach [ENG] and remember that if Brag is a good dog, Holdfast is better [ENG]. Above all, Act honestly and speak boldly [DAN], Tread gently on the ground and leave it as found [ARAP], and If you're in a hole, stop digging [ENG].

FRIENDS AND ENEMIES
finding out who they are

FRIENDS: Be gracious to all men, but choose the best to be your friends [GRE], for A man is known by the company he keeps [ENG]. Listen, for When a stranger cares enough to speak, he becomes a friend [ROM], and make time, for Friendship is a plant which one must water often [GER]. Never forget, There's safety in numbers [ENG], If you play alone on the beach the sea monster will get you [INU], so Two heads are better than one [ENG], and A house can hold a hundred friends [AFR]. Old wine and friends improve with age [ITA], so Of friends the oldest, of everything else the newest [KUR]. Indeed, Nobody should forget old friends and old goats [FAR], maybe because Strangers forgive, friends forget [BUL]. Treat your friends well, If your friend is honey don't lick it all up [EGY], for Friends are lost by calling often or calling seldom [SCO]. Take heed, Many a friend is not known until they are lost [ITA], and remember, a friend accepts another, Warts and all [ENG], because The eyes of a friend do not see the warts [AFG].

GOOD FRIENDS: Life has no blessing like a prudent friend [GRE], for Iron sharpens iron, and one man sharpens another [BIB], so Hold a true friend with both hands [AFR], and remember, A cup of coffee brings forty years of friendship [TUR]. A friend will tell you The world is your oyster [ENG] because Like stars, a friend will guide you [ARAB], just as An old friend is like a saddled horse [AFG], and No camel journey is long in good company [TUR]. A real friend holds your hand in times of distress [AFG], so Share your path with a friend [AFR], for A friend who shares is a friend who cares [ENG], and A friend in need is a friend indeed [ENG]. In fact, Friendship is a single soul dwelling in two bodies [GRE], thus A true friend is like a mirror [IND], so listen to friendly criticism, for Without an opposing wind no kite can fly [CHI].

BAD FRIENDS: Sometimes, New friends can be as deceptive as spring ice [RUS], for Trusting some men is like having water in a sieve [EGY], in other words, If your friend is an ass expect nothing but kicks [IND]. Distance makes the heart grow fonder [ENG], for A hedge between keeps friendships green [GER], but money doesn't: Lend your money and lose your friend [ENG]. Tellingly, A friend to all is a friend to none [GRE], as Everybody's friend is everybody's fool [GER], which is why A man of many companions may come to ruin [BIB], since Bad company ruins good morals [BIB]. So Beware of a man's shadow and a bee's sting [BURM], for Cobras bite, whatever you call them [IND], and If you live in the river then make friends with the crocodile [IND]. Remember, A great talker can be a great liar [FRA], so stay alert, for A friend who leads one astray is an enemy [GRE]; indeed, An insider can bring down a kingdom [IND]. Above all, bear in mind that A wolf with no fangs doesn't lose its hunger [CHI] and Beware of the dog that doesn't bark [NAT AME], he'll be the first to bite [GER],

ENEMIES: All too often Close friends can become close enemies [AFR], for People with the same ideas can be enemies [BURM], so Keep your friends close and your enemies closer [CHI], and never forget, A friend looks you in the eye, an enemy at your feet [KYR], while A wise enemy is better than a foolish friend [AFG]. Generally, you should Eat an enemy for lunch before he has you for dinner [EGY], Use an enemy's hand to catch a snake [PER], and if possible, Give your enemy a hungry elephant [NEP]. Always remember: Faithful are the wounds of a friend; profuse are the kisses of an enemy [BIB], and Wars are easy to start, but hard to end [ROM].

15

FIGHT AND FLIGHT
fortune favors the brave

FIGHT: *Better death before dishonor* [JAP], for *You may as well die fighting as become a slave* [AFR]. *Pick your battles* [ENG], as *A hungry wolf is stronger than a well-fed dog* [UKR] and *Only an ignorant rat will fight a cat* [AFR], however much *Fortune favors the brave* [ENG]. *The bigger they are the harder they fall* [ENG], so *Meet roughness with toughness* [FRA], for *When the going gets tough the tough get going* [AME], and although *Attack is the best defense* [AME], never forget that *One man can guard a narrow pass* [CHI]. Often enough *Showing off is half the fight* [SWA], for you should *Deal gently with the bird you mean to catch* [ITA], as *The greatest victories spill no blood* [CHI] and *There's no need for poison if you can kill with sweets* [IND]. *Keep your eyes open* [ENG] and *Tread carefully* [ENG], for *A thousand good moves are ruined by one bad* [CHI] and *If you have no horse you have no feet* [KYR]. *Avoid chasing cowards lest they become brave* [TUR] and take care, *Loose lips sink ships* [ENG] just as *Ski tracks can be followed* [FIN]. Never forget, *The weakest man can cause hurt* [BURM], and *Blood does not wash out blood* [AFG], so you'll generally find that *If your fist is in his mouth, his fist is in your eye* [YEM]. Remember, *If a man bites a dog it will say he has poor teeth* [SUD], so *Better weight than wisdom you can't carry* [ICE], because *It ain't over till it's over* [AME].

PEACE: Often, *Discretion is the better part of valor* [ENG], so *If you won't bite, don't bare your teeth* [CHI]. Anyway, *The strong don't need clubs* [SEN], for *War is a bad chisel with which to carve out tomorrow* [SIERRA LEONE], and *No war has a cause that reason cannot settle* [ARM]. Wise up, *To live in peace, you must be on good terms with your neighbors* [ZIM], for *Only crows rejoice when grass-hoppers fight* [LESOTHO], so *Better a bad peace than a good war* [HEB]. And hope that *Peace does not need a guard* [SWA], for although *There's strength in unity and*

weakness in division [TAN], *If the lion and the sheep lie down together the sheep won't get any sleep* [KEN]. Bear in mind that *The more you spend on peace, the less you spend on war* [KEN], so *If you can't beat them, join them* [ENG].

FLIGHT: *Evading the enemy takes true courage* [PHIL]; *There are no atheists in foxholes* [AME]. However, although *Tottering is not necessarily falling* [SWA], and sometimes it's true that *Flight is the beginning of collapse* [HEB], at other times *It's better to live a coward than be a dead hero* [ENG], as *He that fights and runs away may live to fight another day* [ENG]. So *Who has no courage must have legs* [ITA], indeed *Fear lends wings* [GER], as *An old man will run through a thorn forest if he is being chased* [AFR], so *Find any port in a storm* [ENG] but remember, *The world's a small place for a fugitive* [KYR]. Why not *Watch and wait* [IND], for *A barking dog seldom bites* [ROM], and *Heroes only appear once the tiger is dead* [BURM].

SUCCESS AND FAILURE
the rough and the smooth

SUCCESS: A good beginning makes a good ending [ITA], just as A small key can open big doors [KUR], and be patient, Great oaks from little acorns grow [ENG], as Bean by bean, the sack gets full [GRE]. Always Take things one step at a time [ENG], because If you go as far as you can see, you'll see further when you get there [PER], which is why The true artist perseveres, whatever his critics say [DUT]. So Hang your clothes in the sunshine [BAS], Keep your eyes on the prize [AME], and Make hay while the sun shines [ENG], because Growing millet doesn't fear the sun [UGA]. Be bold, for Nothing ventured nothing gained [FRA], and Keep your options open [ENG], for The mouse that has but one hole is quickly taken [TUR]. And Don't use an axe to embroider [MALAY] nor a Sledgehammer to crack a nut [ENG], because Succeeds breeds success, in fact Nothing succeeds like success [FRA], even though The bigger a man's head, the greater his headache [PER].

WARNING: Don't count your chickens before they've hatched [ENG], and Don't say hurray until you've jumped the barrier [RUS], for The proof of the pudding is in the eating [ENG], and all too often A water pot only falls off your head when you reach your front door [UGA]. Be prepared too, A reed before the wind lives on while mighty oaks do fall [ENG], and If you want a rose, respect the thorn [PER]. Don't daydream, The road to hell is paved with good intentions [ENG], just as An imaginary mill grinds no flour [BAS], indeed As you make your bed so must you lie on it [EUR], or as they say in America, Garbage in, garbage out [AME]. So bear in mind Success comes from hard work [BAS], as Without working you won't get fish from the pond [RUS], and He who would eat the fruit must climb the tree [SCO]. It's up to you, Failure is the child of neglect [ENG], and If you Snooze you lose [ENG], so If a job's worth doing, it's worth doing well [ENG]. And don't play

too clean, *Nice guys finish last* [AME], or too brash, *A barking dog catches no hares* [EST], or too fast, *Nothing so bold as a blind mare* [SCO]. And *Look before you leap* [ENG] as *Most Shipwrecks happen in unknown waters* [EGY], and *Even good swimmers can sink* [MAD]. Remember too that *You can't unscramble eggs* [AME] and that *You're fine as long as there are no cows on the ice* [DAN].

FAILURE: Chin up! *Failure is the source of success* [CHI], for *Failure teaches you more than success* [RUS], and *He who never fails will never grow rich* [ENG]. Grin and bear it, for you *You can't be a good doctor if you've never been ill* [ARAB], and *Calm seas don't make good sailors* [AFR]. Moreover, *Even the best scribes make blots* [SPA], so learn to *Take the rough with the smooth* [ENG] as often *The obstacle is the path* [ZEN]. All in all, *Life is not a bed of roses* [SPA], for *Where wood is chopped, splinters fly* [POL], but when you do get hurt *Weeping washes the face* [IND]. Therefore *Suffer, suffer, suffer, and you will get the brightest crown* [FIN], and discover along the way that *Adversity makes a strange bedfellow* [ENG].

Richer and Poorer
the best things in life are free

MONEY: If *The best things in life are free* [ENG], why do so many people think that *Money makes the world go round* [AME] and that *Money is power* [AME]? Maybe it's because *He who pays the piper calls the tune* [ENG] and *Money makes dogs dance* [FRA]. Or maybe it's as simple as *Money talks* [ENG], because *Money doesn't grow on trees* [ENG] and *There's no such thing as a free lunch* [AME]. Save it carefully, as *Many a mickle makes a muckle* [SCO], and *A penny saved is a penny earned* [ENG], for *Money has a way of taking wings* [BIB]. Sometimes, though, it's important to spend: *In for a penny, in for a pound* [ENG], they say, but please try to *Get the money honestly if you can* [AME].

RICHER: Watch out, for *When money's not a servant it's a master* [IND], and any gardener will tell you that *Good soil is worth more than gold* [EST]. You may be happier if you *Stay where there are songs* [GYP], and go where *Poor people entertain with the heart* [HAITI], because *It's always the idiots who have money* [EGY], despite the fact that *A fool and his money are soon parted* [ENG]. Remember, *Half of something is better than all of nothing* [ENG], but *Money isn't everything* [ENG], so although *Every bird loves its nest* [ITA], it's funny how *Money can buy you a house, but not a home* [CHI]. And never forget, when you die *You can't take it with you* [ENG], for *You make a living from what you get, you make a life from what you give* [ENG], and *Even the poorest man has the sun and the stars* [FIN].

MODERATION: *Money won't solve all your problems* [SLO], but *Having enough is better than having too much* [BAS] for *The bigger your roof the more snow it collects* [PER], and *Many donkeys mean a lot of hay* [BAS]. Admittedly, there's

One law for the rich, another for the poor [ENG], but More slaves makes more thieves [HEB], so Better a small deal than a long quarrel [NOR], and Better your own copper than another man's gold [GEOR]. That's because Money is the root of all evil [BIB], and When money speaks, the truth stays silent [RUS]. Remember, All that glitters is not gold [RUS], and Pearls are worth nothing in the desert [IND]. You know, A bird wouldn't sing if it knew how poor it is [DAN], so always Count your blessings [AME].

POORER: With no money life can be tough, for The sated do not see the hungry [BAS] and Every rock strikes the feet of the poor [AFG]. Indeed, Beggars can't be choosers [FRA], for a Man with no money can do no nothing in a market [FRA]. Lovers should bear in mind that Love does much, but money does more [FRA] and When money goes out the door, love flies out the window [ENG]. It's the same in Alaska, where Unless you're the lead husky the view stays much the same [INU], because A man with no bread has no authority [TUR], which is why Small fish never sleep [POLY].

21

BEAUTY AND THE BEAST
beauty is but a blossom

BEAUTIFUL: *Beauty is one in a thousand* [TAM], and if you've got it *Beauty is a good letter of introduction* [GER] too. But never forget that *Beauty is but a blossom* [ENG], and that *Beauty is a very fine thing, but you can't live on it* [AME], and in fact *You can't live on beauty, but you can die for it* [SWE]. When more than skin deep, *Beauty is the seasoning of virtue* [POL], indeed *Beauty without virtue is like a rose without scent* [DAN], for *Beauty is but dross if honesty be lost* [DUT]. Some people mystify it: *Beauty is less what one sees than what one dreams* [FLEM], while others struggle with it: *Beauty is the eye's food but the soul's sorrow* [GER], but in most cases *An enemy to beauty is a foe to nature* [ENG] whether or not *Beauty suffers no pain* [IRI]. Beauty can be extended:

If there is light in the soul, there will be beauty in the person. If there is beauty in the person, there will be harmony in the house. If there is harmony in the house, there will be order in the nation. If there is order in the nation, there will be peace in the world [CHI]; and personalized: Beauty is in the eye of the beholder [ENG]. There's no doubt that A beautiful wife keeps a husband busy [IND], just as A handsome husband is common property [AME], and hey, If you're beautiful, whatever you do is fine [ARAB]. But unfortunately, Beauty provokes thieves sooner than gold [ENG], and since Beauty and folly are often companions [FRA] all too often A lazy beauty is fit only for the dunghill [HAW].

BEASTLY: One rotten apple spoils the whole barrel [ENG], so whoever wants to travel far takes care of his beast [FRA] especially since Every beast knows its time [POL]. Take care, Whoever's been bitten by a snake dreads even earthworms [RUS], and so often Under the down-turned bowl there is a smaller one [AFG], so Don't let an angry man wash the dishes [CAMB] and be careful, for Vice is often clothed in virtue's habit [ENG], just as Vices willingly bear the names of virtues [SWE], and Flatterers, like rats, tickle before they bite [MAD]. When dealing with beasts always Know when to cut your losses [ENG], for Thanks won't fill your belly [RUS], and If you know the poison, you may learn how to drink it [ENG]. You could try kissing or killing one, but remember You can't polish a turd [PER], and Reward can be a double edged sword [ARAB], for Honey catches more flies than vinegar [ITA] and all too often Great honors are great burdens [ENG]. A swollen idea can bring ruin [BURM] too, so Don't touch a load you can't lift [AFR], and as A bad penny always turns up [ENG], remember that When the bait costs more than the fish it's time to stop fishing [AFR AME]. Of course, There are few paths without perils [ARM], so Be prepared for conflicts, as they have already begun [TIB] and however good your intention The food you give may come back as poo [AZTEC], so always remember that An ape's an ape, a varlet's a varlet, though they be clad in silk or scarlet [GRE].

LOVE AND LAMENT
written with the eyes

LOVE: Take heed, *One cannot love and be wise* [ROM], for *Love is blind* [ENG], and *Love can make you blind and deaf* [ARAB], as *Love enters man through his eyes and woman through her ears* [POL]. Indeed, *The first love letters are written with the eyes* [FRA] after which *A letter from the heart can be read on the face* [SWA]. *No wind is too cold for lovers* [UKR], and *When one is in love, a cliff becomes a meadow* [ETH], for *Love makes the impossible possible* [IND], and *Love understands all languages* [ROM]. Remember, *The heart sees further than the head* [SWA], which is why *A life with love is happy; a life for love is foolish* [CHI], and it's best to have *One thread for the needle, one love for the heart* [SUD]. Interestingly, *Love can't grow garlic* [ARM], but *Garlic can grow love* [PAK], so put *Food before romance* [JAP], for *The way to a man's heart is through his stomach* [ENG], and *Love has to be shown by deeds not words* [SWA]. Like the sun, *Give more love than you receive* [SWA], for *Love begets love* [ROM] and *A loving heart has no equal* [SWA], indeed *Goodness of heart is more important than appearance* [JAP]. *In love beggar and king are equal* [IND], for *All is fair in love and war* [ENG], and *The heart that loves is always young* [GRE]. Sometimes, *Stolen sugar is the sweetest* [IND], although for many *A mother's love is best of all* [IND]. There's someone for everyone, even *A mended lid for a cracked pot* [JAP], and since *Love makes the world go round* [ENG] of course *Love will find a way* [ENG].

LAMENT: *A broken hand can work but a broken heart can't* [AFG], as all too often, *Those who love us make us cry* [SPA], and *Although you can suffer without love, you can't love without suffering* [GER]. *Love is a despot who spares no one* [NAM], but it's *Better to have loved and lost than never to have loved*

at all [ENG]. In most cases Love hurts but doesn't kill [MEX], so, because The heart knows its own pain [SWA], Pain is obligatory, suffering optional [AME]. Be careful, Yield to your body's desires, and endure the disasters that follow [RUS], for He who marries for love, dies miserably of anger [ITA], so watch out, For a little love you pay all your life [HEB]. Don't be jealous, Diamonds are a girl's best friend [AME], and There is no love without jealousy [ITA], although Jealousy destroys love [MEX], so all too often A loving heart can change to hatred [SWA], and There's no medicine to cure hatred [ASH]. Hate burns its preserver [SWA], so the sooner you Learn to love your enemy [SWA] and realize that Anger is a luxury you can't afford [CHI] the quicker you can Move on [ENG]. Often A lovers' quarrel is love's renewal [ENG] but Many kiss the hand they would love to cut off [SPA], so If you have no big knife, kiss your enemy [SWA]. At the very least Love and let the world know, and hate in silence [DUT].

MARRIED AND SINGLE
halves and wholes

MARRY: *Marry first and love will follow* [ENG], but *Before you marry make sure of a house wherein to tarry* [ENG], for *You should only get married when you can build an igloo* [INU], together if possible, for *Teamwork holds you together, as four eyes see better than two* [GER]. Often, *Girls marry to please parents, widows to please themselves* [CHI], but even so *Marriages are not as they are made, but how they turn out* [ITA]. Thus *If your partner minds the children you'll catch more whales* [INU], and you should *Butcher the animals as your wife directs, as she knows your needs* [INU]. Remember, *Love is a flower which turns into fruit at marriage* [FIN], and much of *Love comes after marriage* [INU], for although *A happy man marries the girl he loves, a happier man loves the girl he marries* [AFR]. This is because *Once the home is set up, love is shown by deeds not words* [SWA], so even if *You only get married when you can sew well* [INU] you'll find that *If you love the vase, you'll love what's inside* [AFR], and that *Children are the reward of life* [AFR].

DALLY: *Love spares no one* [NAM], and *There is Magic in love* [ENG], thus *One wedding often brings another* [ENG]. You should *Follow your heart* [ENG], for *There is no love like the first love* [ITA] and *An early marriage brings long love* [GER], especially since *Marriages are made in heaven* [ENG]. But be aware, *The course of true love never did run smooth* [ENG], so don't *Marry in haste and be sorry at your leisure* [IRI], and *Never choose a spouse by candlelight* [FRA], for *It's much easier to fall in love than to stay in love* [AFR]. Remember, *Pretty paths can be crooked* [CAME], and if you *Marry beauty you marry trouble* [NIG], which is why *A marriage in May is rued for ever* [ROM]. And know that *A kiss must last long enough to be enjoyed* [GRE] and that *Frequent kisses end in a baby* [HUN].

26

SINGLE: Actually, don't get married, *A good marriage lasts three days, bad ones until death* [ITA]; in fact *Marriage is the tomb of love* [RUS], and *Where there is marriage without love, there will be love without marriage* [AME]. Think it over, *Marriage is both heaven and hell* [GER], for *Marriages and ships always need mending* [GRE], as all too often *In marriage cheat who can* [FRA].   Remember, *If you marry a monkey for money, the money goes and the monkey stays* [EGY], so *Never marry for money, as ye'll borrow it cheaper* [SCO] and *Don't marry a woman with bigger feet than yours* [BOT].   *Marry late or never* [ENG], despite the fact that *A late marriage makes orphans* [BELGIAN], but watch out, if you *Always say no* [FRA], you'll see how *The choosy person ends up with the ordinary* [BAS]. *Marriage is a lottery* [ENG], and *A woman's heart is like the autumn sky* [JAP], so do you really want to *Marry and grow tame* [SPA], or be told that *A woman's work is never done* [ENG] or that *A woman's place is in the home* [ENG]? Take heed, *Who marries does well, who marries not does better* [ENG].

CHILDREN AND PARENTS
blood is thicker than water

CHILDREN: *Children are the buttonholes that tie parents together* [ARAB], and since *A child learns what it sees at home* [BAS], often *It takes a whole village to raise a child* [AFR]. Never forget, *Your children are only lent to you* [MOHAWK], which is why *Every child is a certain worry and an uncertain joy* [SWE]. Mostly you get *This cub from that lion* [EGY], for *The apple doesn't fall far from the tree* [ENG], just as *A wild goose never reared a barnyard gosling* [IRI], although *An ill cow can have a good calf* [ENG]. Some *Children are happy when they are fat* [FIN], other *Children should be seen but not heard* [ENG], others are *Early ripe, early rotten* [FRA], so *Spare the rod you spoil the child* [ENG]. Remember, *A son is a son till he gets a wife, a daughter's a daughter for all of her life* [ENG], and often *The eldest son is a blockhead* [JAP] while *The younger brother is the better gentleman* [ENG].

SIBLINGS: *Between brothers accounts should be kept square* [AFG], as *Brothers love each other when they are equally rich* [AFR BAGANDA] but *Where brothers fight a stranger inherits* [AFR IGBO], so often it's safer to *Eat and drink with your brother but have no business* [ALB], for even if *Brothers and sisters are as close as hands and feet* [VIET] it's also true that *Brothers and sisters are the forerunners to strangers* [JAP]. Never forget that *The horns of your sister are horns of gold* [SICILIAN], that *A sin against a sister is an offense against the gods* [AFR] and that *All plants are our brothers and sisters, if we listen* [ARAP].

HOME: *East, west, home is best* [HOL], *Home is where the heart is* [AME], indeed *There's no place like home* [ENG], for *Blood is thicker than water* [ENG], and *Hawks don't pluck out hawks' eyes* [TUR]. *Every hill has its leopard* [AFR HAYA], so *Birds of a feather flock together* [ENG] and remember, *If you create calamity you eat it with* *your family* [AFR], so it's as well to *Wash your dirty clothes at home* [SPA] and *Don't discuss home in the marketplace* [AFR]. *Be a lion at home and a fox abroad* [PER], and never forget that *Charity begins at home* [ENG], *A united family eats from the same plate* [BURU], and *Happy families live on laughter* [IND].

PARENTS: *As God could not be everywhere he made mothers* [HEB], so *You can never repay your debt to your mother* [KURD], which is why *Paradise is under your mother's feet* [ARAB], and *A home without a mother is a desert* [ERITREAN]. Thus *A hungry woman seeks food for her children* [ASH] and *A child carried by its mother doesn't know how far it is to the market* [AFR]. And fathers? Well, *Like father like son* [ENG], except so often when *A thrifty father begets a squandering son* [BAS], so *Father earns, son spends* [JAP]. Maybe it's human nature, *Men may fancy other people's wives but they prefer their own sons* [GEOR], so *When your son grows up, become his brother* [ARAB].

29

HONOR AND SHAME
throne or coffin

HONOR: Honor once lost never returns [DUT], for Honor cannot be bought [PHIL] which is why A good name is the best treasure of all [ITA]. It's Better to be Poor with honor than rich with shame [DUT] and it's also Better to deserve honor and have none, than have honor and not deserve it [POR]. The measure of honor is in the person giving it [HEB], so There's no honor for an eagle in vanquishing a dove [ITA], but There is honor among thieves [ENG] for The thief thinks all men are like himself [SPA]. Do not lose honor through fear [SPA], for A hole is more honorable than a patch [IRE], and Where there is no honor there is no dishonor [POR]. Great honors can be great burdens [ENG] for Honor and reward are in different sacks [POR] so all in all Honor is better than honors [FLEM]. Remember, A prophet is not without honor save in his own country [BIB], so Keep your boasts until after the battle [AFR], for Honor often only blossoms in the grave [FR].

RESPECT: In matters of integrity Honesty is the best policy [ENG], for When a monkey can't reach a ripe banana he says it isn't sweet [SUD], and since We are all guardians of our own honor [IND], If you've only a day to live spend half of it in the saddle [KYR], for it is Better to die on your feet than live on your knees [MEX]. And pay attention, He that respects not is not respected [ENG], so Respect others if you want to be respected [PHIL], because Respect is mutual [ZULU]. Remember, There is no shame in learning [TUR] and If you understand danger you'll not feel it [TUR], which is lucky, as The more the danger, the greater the honor [ENG], for No strength within, no respect without [KASH]. Of course, No one in a shabby coat is treated with respect [ROM] and None but the brave deserve the fair [ENG], so remember, Every slip is not a fall [USA] and it is Better to retire in honor than advance in disgrace [SERB].

SHAME: Shame is complex, *A clean conscience makes a good pillow* [ENG], but *Guilt is good for you* [JAP], for *If you fear shame, you fear sin* [HEB], thus someone *Who fears no shame comes to no honor* [DUT], and *A person with no shame has no conscience* [ENG], as *No sin is hidden to the soul* [IND]. So, *Light a candle rather than curse the darkness* [CHI], and be warned that *A long silence makes a big noise* [AFR]. Take note, *Dirty feet stain the carpet* [TUR] and *Shame lasts longer than poverty* [ENG], so *If you lie down with dogs you'll get up with fleas* [ITAL], just as *One scabby sheep infects a thousand* [ALTAY]; just remember, *Your mouth won't stink if you don't eat garlic* [TUR]. Take note, *A thief's a king until he's caught* [PER], because *Necessity knows no law* [AFR], and sometimes it's just *Either throne or coffin* [IND]. Indeed, *Shame can kill* [PHIL] so *Many lay their shame on the backs of others* [DAN] for *A man with an ill name is half-hanged* [ENG].

31

WORK AND PLAY
come again another day

WORK: Hard work never killed anyone [HEB], although If you can't stand the heat, get out of the kitchen [ENG]. Be prepared to put the hours in [AME], for Work has bitter roots, but sweet fruits [ROMA], and It is working that makes the workman [ENG]. Mind you do it well, Measure seven times and cut once [RUS], for A worker is known by his work [FRA], and Fine work is its own flattery [SLO], so The work praises the workman [GER] if The laborer is worthy of his hire [BIB]. Pick your trade, Aim before you shoot [AFR], Acquire skill and make it deep [HAW], and bear in mind that He who likes his work, to him work comes easy [HEB]. Remember, If you look at the clouds your work will fail [MAYA], just as Weighty work is done with few words [DAN], so Go sure and steady [AME], Haste makes waste [ENG] and A stitch in time saves nine [ENG]; Rome wasn't built in a day [ROM]. Some trade tricks: If you're an anvil be patient, if you're a hammer be strong [KURD], Leap where the hedge is lowest [ITA], and Make a new bucket while you still have the old one [BER]. Never forget, The hardest work is to do nothing [AME], so Everybody must make his own arrows [INU], unless you're a teacher, as He who can does, he who can't teaches [ENG]. Timing is key, Don't put off today's work until tomorrow [AFR], but note, A windy day is not a thatching day [IRI], and Launch the canoe when the breakers are calm [HAW]. Above all, be prepared, A bird caller must always be alert [HAW] just as A cat in gloves catches no mice [FRA]; and remember, Work loves fools [RUS] so A volunteer is worth two pressed men [ENG].

IDLENESS: Idleness is the root of all evil [GER] and Laziness is the mother of all vices [ALB], for The devil makes work for idle hands [ITA]. In addition The lazy pig does not eat ripe pears [ITA], just as Someone with no work in summer has no winter boots [POL], and He who looks for light work goes very tired to bed [HEB].

Excuses are the offspring of laziness [AFR], thus A bad dancer blames the floor [INDO], just as A poor writer blames his pen [SPA] and A bad workman blames his tools [ENG]. However, A bad excuse is better than none [SPA], and If ifs and ands were pots and pans, there'd be no work for tinkers' hands [ENG]. Just remember, You can't get something for nothing [ITA] and If you pay peanuts you get monkeys [AME], or you might even get a Jack of all trades and a master of none [ENG].

PLAY: When the cat is away the mice will play [ENG], since All work and no play makes Jack a dull boy [ENG], so don't Burn the candle at both ends [FRA] as It's the pace that kills [ENG], and hear this: An hour of play is worth more than a year of talking [POR]. So it's Better to play for nothing than to work for nothing [SCO] although If you work like an ant you'll eat sugar [YEM]. It's nearly always best if you Don't roll up your trousers before you reach the stream [KUR] and bear in mind that Barbers don't shave their own beards [AFR]. In any case, There's a time and place for everything [ENG], so Don't forget to breathe [AME].

CAREFUL AND CAREFREE
patience is a virtue

CAUTION: Take care, Curiosity killed the cat [ENG] like A wandering hen is food for the fox [BAS], so especially When the fox is being charming, watch your chickens [BAS], as it's best to Be wise before rather than after [NOR]. And Don't put all your eggs in one basket [ENG], for just as You never see a peacock dance in a wood [IND], you should Never stand in front of a judge or behind a donkey [IND] or Try to stop a donkey that isn't yours [AFG]. Always Keep your cards close to your chest [ENG] and Keep your wounded arm inside your cloak [EGY], for it's Better to lose an anchor than a ship [DAN], which is why Two anchors keep a vessel secure [FRA]. Don't bid for fish that haven't been caught [IND] and remember that A bird in the hand is worth ten in the bush [INDO], for in the end He who laughs last laughs best [FRA]. Remember too, Caution is no cowardice; even fleas are armed [RUS], which is why you should Trust in God, but tie up your camel [PER].

PATIENT: Go One step at a time [ENG] for Hurry hurry has no blessings [SWA], and Patience is the mother of a beautiful child [AFR BANTU], just as Don't care was made to care [ENG] and Diligence grows into brilliance [INDO]. Patience is a virtue [FRA], although sometimes Patience is the virtue of asses [FRA], but Patience can cook a stone [AFR], and Patience can extract sweetness from soreness [LEB]. In fact Patience is the key to all things [PER], for Patience is the greatest prayer [IND] and If you don't have patience you can't make beer [AFR]. To sum up, Begin with patience, and end with pleasure [SWA], in other words Go slow and steady [ICE] as Good things come to those who wait [FRA]. And If you can't be good, be careful [AFR], for Carefulness can go everywhere [CHI], although Be careful what you wish for, you might just get it [ENG]. Know too that He who takes no care of little things will not have the care of great ones [GER].

CAREFREE: *Those who don't dream are lost* [AB AUS], so sometimes you have to *Throw caution to the wind* [ENG] because *Worry is the interest paid by those who borrow trouble* [AME], and *A day of worry is more exhausting than a week of work* [AME]. Indeed, *Care brings gray hairs* [ROM] and *Worry, not work, kills a man* [MALI]. So *Put off your worries for the morrow* [HEB], *Where there's life there's hope* [GRE], and *Live to eat* [CAT], for *Worries are easier to bear with soup than without it* [HEB]. And *Eat to live* [GRE] too, for in the end *One is what one eats* [GER] and *Everyone has their own way of eating yoghurt* [TUR], so *Live for today* [CHI], say *Easy come, easy go* [ITA], *C'est la vie!* [FRA] or *Today me, tomorrow thee* [ENG], and aim to *Be first at the feast, last at the fight* [IND]. However, *It's a brave bird that makes its nest in the cat's ear* [IND], and *When a fox is lame the rabbit still jumps* [NAT AME], but if you worry that *Calm comes after a storm* [ENG] then just remember, *Not enough problems? Get a goat* [ARAB].

EXCESS AND DEFICIENCY
wilful waste makes woeful want

EXCESS: Often, *Your eyes are bigger than your belly* [DUT] and, since *Your desires go as far as your eyes can see* [BAS], you end *Up to your neck in pleasure, up to your eyes in grief* [IND], as *Every excess develops into a vice* [ROM]. So *Nothing to excess* [ROM], instead *Don't bite off more than you can chew* [ENG], for *After the feast comes the reckoning* [AME]; *The things you don't need will kill you* [AFR TUAREG]. Unfortunately, *If you have much you need much* [BAS], which is why *Wine has drowned more people than the sea* [FRA], so even if you strike it rich *Only eat an elephant one bite at a time* [ASH] and keep on reminding yourself that *You can't have your cake and eat it* [ENG], as *Where there's sugar there will be ants* [MALAY]. Remember, *After dinner rest awhile, after supper walk a mile* [ROM].

BALANCE: Try as you might, *You can't turn a millwheel with a pail of water* [TUR], and even if you *Try to paper over the cracks* [ENG] *A liar's candle won't last the night* [TUR]. So *Look on the bright side* [ENG] for *There's a high tide after every ebb* [SUD] and since *The best things come in small packages* [FRA], be glad that *Enough is as good as a feast* [ENG], because *The more you know the less you need* [AB AUS]. For *a long life be healthy not fat, drink like a dog and eat like a cat* [GER], *Follow moderation in all things* [GRE], and cheer up, *Squirrels that eat dried chapattis do not know what sugar tastes like* [IND]. In the end, it's *Better to have a small fish than an empty bowl* [ENG] and *Better the gravy than no grease at all* [AFR AME] so remember, *If you don't have what you love, you must love what you have* [FRA], as *Luxury begins when you start wearing shoes* [TUAREG]. In fact, *Appetite comes from eating* [SPA] and *Hunger is the best sauce* [FRA] so be careful, *Coriander is good, but not too much* [SPA]. Although *Many hands make light work* [ENG], it's also true that *Too many cooks spoil the broth* [ENG] and *Too many butchers ruin the cow* [AFG], so *Before eating take time to thank the food* [ARAP], and don't forget, *Today's egg is better than tomorrow's hen* [TUR].

DEFICIENCY: Don't tell your guests that *A warm fire is better than a good meal* [AFG], for *If you hide good food from your guests it will turn into worms* [MAYA] just as *An empty drum makes the loudest noise* [INDO] and *An empty cellar makes an angry butler* [DAN]. *Man cannot live by bread alone* [ENG], and despite the fact that *Hunger will change beans into almonds* [ITA] and *Hunger is the best cook* [ROM], *Hunger is a poor advisor* [MEX] and *Hunger sharpens anger* [ROM]. In the end *You can't amuse a hungry person* [AFR], for *Fine words don't butter parsnips* [ENG], which is why *An army marches on its stomach* [EUR] and *A hungry dog does not fear the stick* [ITA]; *It's the shy who die of hunger* [ALB]. Remember, *Cheap meat smells cheap when you boil it* [ARAB], *Cheap mutton has no fat* [KYR] but *Old hens make the best soup* [MEX]. And never forget that *An empty calabash does not sink* [AFR], just as *An empty house is full of noise* [SWISS].

LUCKY AND HAPLESS
make your own

CHANCE: Beware, Do not entrust to an hour's chance what you have earned in a lifetime [SPA], for He that leaves certainty and sticks to chance, when fools pipe he may dance [FRA], indeed If you forsake certainty and depend on an uncertainty, you will lose both the certainty and the uncertainty [IND]. In fact The only certainty is uncertainty [ROM], as Fortune is as fickle as she is fair [GER], so often Luck, like glass, shines and breaks [ROMA], as Fortune and flowers do not last forever [CHI]. Since Luck and ill luck are neighbors [NOR] it can seem as though All is good luck or bad luck in this world [FRA]. However, One man's loss is another's gain [ENG] and in fact Each person is the architect of their own fortune [ROM], so You make your own luck [AME], especially if you Count not what is lost, but what remains [CHI], because No snowflake falls in the wrong place [ZEN]. Haven't you ever noticed How often things occur by chance, for which we dared not even hope [ROM]?

LUCKY: Luck is magical, An ounce of luck is worth a pound of wisdom [ENG], indeed With luck everything is possible [HEB], and of course Luck leads the bride [DAN]. Does Luck comes to those who look for it [SPA], or is it that A person does not seek luck, luck seeks a person [TUR]? Many folk Touch wood for luck [ENG], say Third Time lucky [ENG], or hold that Odd numbers bring luck [ROM], but maybe it's as simple as: For good luck sleep and wake [JAP]. They say Diligence is the mother of good luck [ARAB], but also There's luck in leisure [ENG], so relax, Good luck is better than early rising [IRI] and Fortune comes to a smiling house [JAP]. That said, To wait for luck is to wait for death [JAP], for One must lose a worm to catch a fish [CHI]; indeed The world belongs to the bold [SPA] and If you throw a handful of stones, at least one will hit [IND]. Also, take heed, Need makes people better, good luck makes them worse [HEB], and Nothing is worse than being accustomed to good fortune [ROM], for Luck sometimes comes without blemish, but never without a catch [GER]; remember that, when Luck knocks at the door and inquires whether prudence is within [DAN]. But nevertheless, If luck comes let it find your door wide open [SPA], for luck has but a slender anchorage [DAN]. And remember, luck never gives; it only lends [SCO] and Fortune cannot take away what she did not give [ROM].

HAPLESS: If ill-fortune strikes, even jelly will break your teeth [PER], just as An unlucky person finds bones in his tripe dinner [EGY], and On the day a monkey is to die all the trees are slippery [AFR]. In the same way Bread always falls on the buttered side [ENG], and It never rains but it pours [ENG]. Some people have all the luck [ENG], others don't, Luck sometimes visits a fool, but never sits down with him [DAN], and The more honest a man the worse his luck [GER], but watch out, Don't store milk in a sieve and complain of bad luck [AFG]. While There is seldom a single wave [ICE] and Bad luck comes by pounds and goes away by ounces [ITA], it's also true that No storm lasts for ever [SPA], so Luck will turn [AME]. Indeed He that has no bad luck grows weary of good luck [SPA], as You Learn more by losing than winning [AFR]. So remember, Bad luck is good for something [FRA], as When a big tree falls goats can eat its leaves [AFR].

HOPE AND DESPAIR
silver linings

HOPE: Hope springs eternal [DAN], thus Every cloud has a silver lining [ENG], and Tomorrow is another day [ENG], for In the land of hope there is no winter [CHI]. Don't worry, If the sky falls we'll catch the larks [ENG], and If you die today you'll not sin tomorrow [YEM], so There's hope while your fishing-line is still in the water [NOR]. Live in hope [ENG], God will find a low branch for the bird that can't fly [KUR], so just Follow the river and you'll get to the sea [IND]. Hope keeps us alive [FRA], despite the fact that Hope is the mother of fools [POL], and He that lives on hope has a slender diet [SCO]. You know, even Crooked logs make straight fires [FRA] and Even foul water will quench a fire [MON], so Persevere and never fear [ENG], for the person Who digs lives [AUSTRIA] although Those who are declared dead live longer [GER]. Remember, A long hope is sweeter than a short surprise [HUNG], just as Hope keeps the poor alive, while fear kills the rich [FIN].

CONTENTMENT: Hope for the best and prepare for the worst [ENG], for it's Better to be one-eyed than blind [GER]. And Don't worry about tomorrow, because you don't know what may happen to you today [HEB]; Time will tell [GRE], Time is a great healer [GRE], Enjoy yourself, it's later than you think [CHI]. Also, Don't worry about unlaid eggs [GER], for Worrying never did anybody any good [SWE], instead Face your fears [ENG], for The death of fear is doing what you dread [SEQUICHIE]. In fact, Fear and hope are the parents of God [AZTEC] so if God doesn't need our prayers [AFG], at least Don't throw the baby out with the bathwater [ENG] but Be content with what God has given you [PHIL], for He has enough who is content [FRA]. Cross a bridge when it comes [ENG], and remember, Who hides his grief finds no remedy [TUR]. As men fear snakes, snakes fear men [TIB], thus Every why has a wherefore [FRA], and Your feet take you where your heart lies [AFG].

DESPAIR: Just as *Every rose has a thorn* [ENG], *Despair and hope are sisters* [SLO], so *He who hopes despairs* [ROM].   No *lamp burns until morning* [PER], thus *Shadows grow in moonlight* [CHI], but never forget that *The darkest hour is just before dawn* [ENG].   *Bad news travels fast* [ENG], for *Bad news is its own horse* [BAS], just as *Hunger drives the wolf out of the forest* [FRA] and *A bleating kid excites the wolf* [ENG].   Be prepared, *Misfortunes never come singly* [FRA], *After one loss come many* [FRA], and *Not all the buds on a bush will blossom* [IND].   You're on your own, for *Good fortune seldom knocks twice* [ENG] and *Most prayers go unanswered* [NOR], so take care you don't *Live by hope and die of hunger* [ITA], as *Grief is to the soul what a worm is to wood* [TUR].   However much *Despair gives courage to a coward* [ENG], remember *Despair never pays debts* [AME], and *You can't put out a fire with spit* [ARM].   And *Pent up grief will burst the heart* [ITA], so when *New grief awakens the old* [ENG], instead *Drown your grief in pleasure* [EGY].

41

STASIS AND CHANGE
the same river

STASIS: Only the wisest and the stupidest of men never change [CHI], for When you're finished changing, you're finished living [AME]. Old habits die hard [ENG], and Regret always comes too late [ITA], but It's no use crying over spilled milk [ENG], for you'll find It's just the same dog with a different collar [SPA], as Change alone is unchanging [GRE]. Therefore, although A leopard can't change its spots [ENG] and A dog's tail never straightens [EGY], The more things change the more they stay the same [GRE], for Nothing is carved in stone [ITA], and Never is a long time [ENG]. Take care [ENG] you Mind what you wish for [ENG], although If wishes were horses beggars would ride [ENG], and if you do Set a beggar on a horse he'll ride to the devil [ENG]; therefore be sensible, The dog only bites when you tread on its tail [CAME] so If it ain't broke don't fix it [AME], and Don't change horses in midstream [ENG]. Bear in mind that The past is the past [JAP], and When a man is out of sight the land remains [MAORI], for Beneath a lying stone no water flows [RUS], though Water flows but the stones remain [JAP].

CHANGE: It's never too late to change [GER], and A change is as good as a rest [ARAB]. That's why A squeaking wheel gets the grease [ENG], and A change of pasture makes fat calves [ENG], but remember that To change and to change for the better are two different things [GER]. Of course, Every action has its opposite [ENG], so When the wind is great, bow before it [CHI] and Let the wind choose the canoe's speed [SAM], for When the music changes so does the dance [AFR], or as the Scots say: Change of masters change of manners [SCO]. Therefore, Let the water you don't need flow [SPA], for All is flux, nothing stays still [GRE], and You can't step into the same river twice [GRE], as Nature admits of no permanence [ENG]. Some say Let it be worse as long as it is change [HEB], for If anything can

go wrong it will [ENG], however *The rain falls on more than one roof* [CAME], and *What was hard to bear can be sweet to remember* [IND]. Therefore, *Go with the flow* [KOR], but be careful, *Without the forest there will be no water, and without water there will be no rice* [MAD], although *If you wait long enough even eggs grow legs* [ETH]. Remember that *Many a sudden change takes place on a spring day* [IRI], so *Seize the day* [ROM] and always bear in mind that all life on Earth has to *Adapt or perish* [ENG].

POWER AND HUMILITY
a bee among flowers

RULING: *People follow the ways of their kings* [ARAB], thus *A king and a crying child have their way* [JAP], unless *The mountains are high and the emperor is far away* [CHI]. Take heed, *The one who knows not how to dissemble, knows not how to rule* [ROM], and also know that *Every monarch is subject to a mightier one* [ROM], just as *Every power is subject to another power* [AFR SHONA], so *Rule the mountains to rule the river* [FRA]. Remember too that *Eagles don't catch flies* [DUT] and *Lions don't turn round when small dogs bark* [AFR], but *A little force can move large masses* [ICE]. Bear in mind that *Only billy goats are born to be masters* [NOR] and *Power often goes before talent* [DAN], so *A good king is better than an old law* [DAN].

HARD POWER: Alas, *The best apples are eaten by the bears* [TUR], for *Peace does not make a good ruler* [AFR], instead *Might makes right* [GRE], for *Pull someone by their ears and their head will follow* [IND], and *Flies don't land on a boiling pot* [ITA]. *Only a hand that can wield a sword may hold a scepter* [UZB], but *Much power makes many enemies* [ENG], and *No matter how big the whale a harpoon can kill him* [MALAY]. So, *He who continually uses an axe must keep it sharp* [AFR HAUSA], and *If a nail sticks up it is hammered down* [JAP], just as *A head on a spike no longer conspires* [NORSE]. Thus, while he *Who owns the stick will own the buffalo* [IND], in the end *He who lives by the sword dies by the sword* [BIB], and *When the tree falls, the monkeys scatter* [CHI].

SOFT POWER: *A good sword can keep others in their scabbards* [DAN], but it's also true that *The pen is mightier than the sword* [ENG], for *With sweet words you can lead an elephant* [PER], and in any case *The queen bee rarely stings* [POR]. Of course, *If you want obedience then only command the possible* [ARAB], and aim to delegate, for *Absolute power corrupts absolutely* [ENG]. Also, try to *Take out your anger on the saddle, not the donkey* [BAS], as *Zeal without prudence is frenzy* [ENG]. And observe too that *An honest magistrate has lean clerks* [CHI], as *A little with honesty is better than a great deal with knavery* [ENG].

HUMILITY: *He who has not served cannot command* [ENG], so *Don't forget what it is to be a sailor when you're a captain* [TAN]; *Cap in hand never did any harm* [ITA]. Inevitably, *Too humble is half proud* [HEB], and *Pride comes before a fall* [ENG], so *If you're on an elephant don't imagine there's no dew on the grass* [AFR], as *Even the tallest tree has an axe at its foot* [KURD] and *A small thistle still stings* [GRE]. Wherever you are, *There's always room at the top* [AME], for *No mountain is tall enough to block out the sun* [CHI], and *If the mountain won't come to Muhammad, Muhammad must go to the mountain* [ENG], for *A ruler is his people's servant* [YEM]. Aim to *Be a bee among flowers, not a fly on a trash-heap* [INDO], never forget that *We only borrow the earth from our children* [NAT AME], and that *Great trees afford wonderful shade* [CHI].

45

TRUE AND FALSE
and whose fault

TRUTH: *Truth is heavy, so few men carry it* [HEB], indeed *A truth-teller finds all doors closed* [DAN], for *Whoever tells the truth will be chased out of nine villages* [AFR], but still, it's *Better to suffer for truth than prosper by falsehood* [DAN]. *A true word needs no oath* [TUR], though *Many a true word is spoken in jest* [ENG] just as *The worst insults are true* [BAS]. *Ask the truth from a child* [AFG], as *Whatever is in the heart will come to the tongue* [PER], but be ready, *Nothing hurts like the truth* [ENG]; indeed it's best to *Speak the truth with one foot in the stirrup* [IND], for *Truth is time's daughter* [SPA]. Luckily, *There is truth in wine* [GRE] for *The Truth lies at the bottom of a well* [GRE]. All too often though, *Truth is the*

first casualty of war [AME], as The truth is half a quarrel [IND]. Remember, Every fable is a bridge to truth [ARAB] but Truth is stranger than fiction [ENG], so Don't ask questions of fairy tales [HEB]; Not everything that is true is to be discussed [SPA].

FAULTS: A fault confessed is half-redressed [AFR], whereas A fault once denied is twice committed [FRA], for To justify a fault is a second fault [ROM]. Remember, Even a good man has his faults [ENG], so Deal with the faults of others as gently as with your own [CHI]. Also be aware that Faults are thick when love is thin [DAN], and also that A man who falls into a well will seize even the edge of a sword [HAUSA] because Falling is easier than rising [IRI], so Don't look where you fell, but where you slipped [LIBERIAN].

LIES: Some liars tell the truth [ARAB], but even so, A half-truth is a whole lie [HEB] and A thousand probabilities do not make one truth [ITA]. Indeed, A little truth makes the whole lie pass [ITA], for Art conceals art [ROM]; but still, You can't ride two horses at once [ENG], just as You can't serve God and Mammon [ENG]. Remember, Until the lion can talk, men's tales will laud the hunter [AFR] and A pedlar always praises his wares [SPA], so even though Seeing is believing [ENG], A man with a big knife is not always a good cook [DAN], especially since What comes on the table must be eaten [GER]. Your mind can lie to you, for Even if your enemy is only an insect he will look like an elephant [TUR], and bear in mind that The eyes do not see what the mind does not want [IND]. So If you must lie then have a good memory [ARAB] for If you tell a lie in the next town it will be home before you [BAS]. Even if A lie has no author [IND], The smallest lies are deadly spears [AFR YORUBA], Falsehood travels and grows [DAN], and despite the fact that A lie has little legs [ENG], A lie will run halfway round the world before the truth has got its boots on [ENG]. Never forget, A guilty conscience is a powerful enemy, for the guilty person has the higher voice [NEP], so It's often best to keep your head down [ENG] and just accept that Everybody lies, apart from my mother and father [BER].

STRONG AND WEAK
small fish grow big

STRONG MIND: *Strength is defeated by strategy* [PHIL] so *Being wise is better than being strong* [BIB], for *You don't have to cut a tree down to get its fruit* [CAMB]. Understand that *The strength of the bee is its patience* [WEI], so *Be master of mind, rather than mastered by mind* [JAP], and realize that *The forest needs the tiger just as the tiger needs the forest* [CAMB]. Know too that *Silence is a source of great strength* [CHI], and that *Our strength grows out of our weakness* [AME], in fact even *The weakness of the enemy makes our strength* [NAT AME], because *That which does not kill us makes us stronger* [GER]. Even so, *There's no point in an umbrella if your shoes leak* [IRI], for *You don't stumble over a mountain, but you do over a stone* [IND], so *Call the bear Uncle until you are over the bridge* [ROMA], and bear in mind *You can't clap with one hand* [AFG]. Remember, *He who acts honestly acts bravely* [ROM], and *A brave man gets his reward* [IRI], so *Plan your year in the spring, your day at dawn* [CHI], for *Fuel alone will not light a fire* [CHI].

STRONG BODY: Be strong, for *Only the strong will survive* [JAM], but *Attempt nothing beyond your strength* [ROM], for *It is the overload that kills* [SPA], as *Even the strongest eagles can't fly beyond the stars* [INU] and *Even horses die from hard work* [RUS]. Note that *You can only lean against something strong* [IND], which is why *A buffalo doesn't feel the weight of his horns* [IND], and just as *Big fish eat little fish* [ENG], *Little fish grow big* [FRA]. And *The strength of fish is in the water* [AFR SHONA] for *A river is made drop by drop* [AFG] and *A steady drop will carve the stone* [GER]. So persevere, *No pain no gain* [ENG], and *Where there's a will there's a way* [ENG], for *Big fleas have little fleas upon their backs to bite them* [IRI], and *If you ride a camel you need not fear dogs* [BER]. Remember that *A cat is a lion in her own lair* and also that *An arch never sleeps* [IND].

WEAKNESS: A *chain is only as strong as its weakest link* [ROM], and *Who is brave enough to tell a lion that his breath smells* [BER]? Alas, *To the mediocre, mediocrity appears great* [IND], so *Weak souls always set out to work at the wrong time* [FRA] and *The weak go to the wall* [ENG]. Of course, *Every little helps* [FRA], because *A little help is better than a lot of pity* [IRI], but still, *Fleas jump on sickly dogs* [SPA] and *The cord breaks at last by the weakest pull* [SPA] so mind you *Hate not the man, but the weakness* [ICE], and *Endure the weaknesses of others by knowing your own* [JAP]. Remember, *A bully is always a coward* [ENG] and *A viper without fangs is a piece of rope* [IND], so *Make a weak man your enemy not your friend* [RUS] and *Keep your broken arm inside your sleeve* [CHI]. Bear in mind that *When the wine is in the wit is out* [ENG], so *It's better to limp than be footless* [NOR], and always *Better to stay on land than to cry for help from the water* [NOR].

KIND AND SELFISH
good turns

KIND: *Generosity is wealth* [AFR], they say, and *Kindness is even better than piety* [HEB], for *Altruism is the mark of a superior being* [EGY], and indeed *Kindness is the soul's best quality* [CHI], as *Kindness nourishes both giver and receiver* [AFR]. So *Kindness is not just for the sake of others* [JAP] because *If you sow kindness you reap gratitude* [ARAB], and *Kindness begets kindness* [GRE] as *One good turn deserves another* [ENG]. So *Even if life is short, a smile only takes a second* [CUBA] and certainly, *A good word never broke a tooth* [IRI], thus *A word of kindness is better than a fat pie* [ENG], and even if you're hungry *Don't go where the food is plentiful but where the people are kind* [BOT]. *Forget injuries but never a kindness* [CHI], indeed *Write injuries in the sand, kindnesses in marble* [FRA], except *A forced kindness deserves no thanks* [ENG]. Bear in mind too that *Kindness is remembered, meanness is felt* [HEB], so *A kindness is easily forgot, an unkindness never* [IND], and be aware that *The sandal tree perfumes the axe that fells it* [IND].

TOO KIND: *Yours truly is not always true* [ENG], and *Too much kindness can lead to tiredness* [SWISS], for often *The kind hearted becomes a slave* [BURM], particularly if there is *Too much kindness but not enough gratitude* [TUR]. Just be aware that *There is no honey without gall* [SPA], so *Speak softly but carry a big stick* [AFR], and recall that the *The hand of compassion is stung when it strokes a scorpion* [PER]. Also be aware that *To lend is to buy trouble* [IND], for *He that goes a-borrowing, goes a-sorrowing* [ENG], as *The greatest humiliation is helplessness* [EGY] so *Try to be envied rather than pitied* [GRE]. Remember, *He who depends on himself will attain the greatest happiness* [CHI] because *He travels fastest who travels alone* [ENG], so generally *It is better to buy than to receive* [JAP], especially as *The buyer's eyes are in the seller's hands* [ITA].

SELFISH: *No one calls on a miser* [YORUBA], because *Asking a miser for help is like trying to dig through seawater* [ARM], just as *A dog with a bone knows no friends* [DUT]. Indeed, *What you have, hold* [ENG], for *It is better to save than to beg* [BAS], for *Desire has no rest* [ENG] and *A person's desire grows day by day* [HEB]. However, *All suffering is caused by desire* [CHI]. so *Grasp all and you lose all* [ENG], as *Gluttony kills more than the sword* [ENG] and *A glutton young becomes a beggar old* [ENG]. Or you can *Buy, buy, buy, and let the children pay the debts* [FIN], for *A selfish person will even take advantage of wind and clouds* [JAP]. But *He who has much is afraid of many* [SPA], which is why *Greed keeps men poor* [MON], so *Don't be a slave to your desires* [ENG], but know that *All that is not given is lost* [IND] and *No man is an island* [ENG]. Remember, *The miser's bag is never full* [DAN], and *Coffin carriers love the plague* [JAP], but miser or not, *After three days guests and fish smell* [IND], and *The guest who breaks the dishes is not*

YOUNG AND OLD
old dogs and new tricks

YOUNG: *You're only young once* [AME] so *Make the most of it* [ENG], *The world is your oyster* [ENG], although *Those whom the gods love die young* [GRE]. *Everything new is beautiful* [ITA], though *Nothing is so new it has not happened before* [DAN], so *Youth is the time to sow* [GER], for *The vigor of youth passes away like a spring flower* [ROM], yes, *Youth slips away as water from a sandy shore* [IRI]. *You have to learn to walk before you can run* [ENG], but *Green twigs bend easily* [TUR] so *Instructing the young is like engraving stone* [MOROCCAN], just as *The young cock crows as he hears the old one* [YORUBAN], for *What youth learns, age does not forget* [DAN]. *A new broom sweeps clean* [ENG], and *Diligent youth makes easy age* [ITA], but beware, *Young saint, old devil* [ENG]. In fact, *Youth is wasted on the young* [ENG], for many *Mysterious roads beckon to young people* [ANGOLA], indeed *Youth, ignorance, and impatience ruin people* [ARAB], and *Young folks think old folks fools, while old folks know the young are* [GER]. *You can't put an old head on young shoulders* [DAN], so *Never send a boy to do a man's job* [ENG], but remember, *When a palm branch reaches its height it must make way for a young one* [NIG], for *There is always something new out of Africa* [GRE].

OLD: *Walnuts and pears you plant for your heirs* [ENG], but *Old age comes for free* [NOR], so *The young rely on their parents, the old on their children* [VIET]. *Youth has a beautiful face, old age a beautiful soul* [SWE], for *Young twigs may be bent, but not old trees* [DUT]. *Elderliness is a richness* [BURU], so *An old man is put in a boat to give advice, not to row* [UGA], for *Taught by necessity, old people know a lot* [BAS]. *You don't teach the forest paths to an old gorilla* [AFR] any more than you'd *Teach your grandmother how to suck eggs* [ENG], indeed *Many a good tune is played on an old fiddle* [IRI] so *Cherish youth but trust old age* [PUEBLO], for it's *Better to be an old* man's darling than a young man's slave [ENG]. And even though *Old cows like young grass* [BURM], *It's better to have an old spouse than none* [TAN], for *A man grows old but his courage remains* [KYR]. *Young barber, old physician* [ENG], they say, for *We grow old fast, but wise only slowly* [CHI], for *Age doesn't make you wise, but it does make you slow* [FIN]. Of course, *Young men can die, but old men must* [ROM] for *When a lion grows old the flies attack him* [TAN] which is why *Old women get uneasy when dry bones are mentioned* [AFR], as *Old age leads to something worse* [NOR]. However, *Nobody is so old that he doesn't think he'll live for another year* [ROM], so even if *You can't teach an old dog new tricks* [ENG], *As we grow old our bad qualities keep us young* [FIN]. But it's also true that *Old sins cast long shadows* [ENG] so although *Everyone has seen a cradle, nobody knows their grave* [NOR].

HEALTH AND SICKNESS
an apple a day

HEALTH: *A healthy mind lives in a healthy body* [ROM], indeed *A healthy mind makes a healthy body* [JAP], which is why *A person's health is in his feet* [IRI]. *Good health is the sister of beauty* [MALT], so *He who would be healthy, let him be cheerful* [WEL], for *Health is better than wealth* [ENG]. Of course, *When you're busy you are never ill* [JAP], because *Regularity is the best medicine* [IND], but *Life is uncertain, so eat the dessert first* [FIN], for *It's all one whether you die of illness or love* [ITA]. Often, *Health is only valued when sickness comes* [ENG], as *Illness gives you a taste for health* [HUN], so remember, *Prevention is better than cure* [GER]. *An apple a day keeps the doctor away* [ENG], but *Water is the oldest medicine*

[FIN], so *Take good care of the well* [SWA]. Never forget, *Have a clean heart and you may walk near the altar* [GRE], for *If the heart be stout, a mouse can lift an elephant* [TIB], but even *The stoutest heart must fail at last* [AME], so *Your health comes first, you can hang yourself later* [HEB].

HEALING: *Laughter is the best medicine* [AZE], just as *A library is medicine for the mind* [GRE] and *Minor complaints are cured by eating* [FIN]. Otherwise, *The sauna is the poor man's pharmacy* [FIN], as *It's better to sweat than to sneeze* [SPA]. *Feed a cold, starve a fever* [AME], and bear in mind *The medicine that hurts does you good* [SWA]. Don't worry, *For every ailing foot there is a slipper* [BRA], so *Don't hide the truth from your lawyer or your physician* [ROM] as *Hiding sickness prevents a cure* [SWA]. *Every patient is a doctor after his cure* [IRI], but mind, *Before healing others, heal yourself* [AFR] and then *Scratch people where they itch* [ENG]. *Console a sufferer, even an enemy* [SWA], and remember *There is no cure for old age* [SWA], despite the fact that *A creaking door hangs longest* [ENG].

SICKNESS: *Nothing tastes good to the sick* [SPA], as *Illness starts with the mouth* [JAP], and *Sickness comes in haste and leaves at leisure* [DAN]. *Sickness is everyman's master* [DAN], indeed *Sickness is our common lot* [ENG], for *Neither hat nor crown help against headache* [SWE], and *We are all in the laps of the gods* [GRE]. *If Sickness is awful, a relapse is worse* [SICILIAN], which is why *The worst ache is the present ache* [LEB], and *Mortals bear many ills* [ROM]. *Desperate ills require desperate remedies* [FRA], and *If sauna, liquor and tar don't help, the disease is fatal* [FIN]. Note that *An imaginary illness is even worse than a real one* [HEB], because *Those whom the gods would destroy they first make mad* [GRE]. It's odd how *Sickness is felt, but health not at all* [ENG], so maybe *An illness tells us what we are* [ITA], which is why it's *Better to have a sick body than an ignorant mind* [GRE]. Remember, *No one buys illness with money* [LAT], for *Sickness is the physician's feast* [IRI], and *If you eat caribou hair, you get an itchy bottom* [INU].

LIFE AND DEATH
from home to home

LIFE: Life is a dream, but don't wake me [HEB], Life is but a bubble [GRE], Life is like licking honey from a thorn [HUNG]. Life is the flash of a firefly [NAT AME], so Nobody is quick enough to live life to the full [SPA]. Even so, try to Live life to the full [SWE], for As we live, so we learn [HEB], and Art is long and life is short [GRE], thus A good life keeps away wrinkles [SPA]. Life has its ups and downs [AME], for Life would be too smooth if it had no rubs in it [ENG], but It is one life, whether we spend it laughing or weeping [JAP], so remember, Life is for one generation; a good name is forever [JAP]. A person is lent, not given, life [ROM] so Live until you die, and don't panic [BAS]. Indeed, Live and let live [ENG], and Fear life, not death [RUS], for Living is harder than dying [PHIL], and He that fears death lives not [ENG] so Don't die before you die [PER]. Or perhaps do Die before you die [AFG], for Life is sweet [ENG], and What does the blind man know of the lotus flower's beauty [IND]? With A precipice in front of you, wolves behind you, such is life [ROM], therefore Live so the world will cry when you die and you'll rejoice [CHEYENNE]. Remember, The less you sleep, the more you get out of life [HEB], also Being thin is not death [BEMBA], and Bad breath is better than no breath at all [AME].

DEATH: Despite the fact that Birth is the remedy for death [AFR], There's no cure for old age [SWA], and One is certain only of death [HEB], just as The top of a tall tree will soon be firewood [BURM]. Approaching death is great, you just give up [FIN], so don't worry, Death kills worry [LAT] anyway, and When death is there, dying is over [RUS]. Mercifully, A nose doesn't smell its own head rotting [IND] and You only die once [POR], for Death is concise, like a good proverb [RUS]; Death is the great leveller [ROM]. Indeed, In death, everyone is equal [PHIL], as Death alone measures equally [CZE], yes Death combs us all with the same comb [SWE]. Death

devours lambs as well as sheep [ENG], Death can carry a fat tsar as easily as a lean beggar [RUS], Death takes the poor man's cow and the rich man's child [FRA]. Death regards spring as winter [RUS], for Death keeps no calendar [ENG], and since Death rides a fast camel [ARAB], it's Best to send a lazy messenger to the angel of death [HEB]. Often, You only become important after death [HEB], but if There are skeletons in the closet [PHIL], you'll find Death is the revealer of secrets [AFR HAUSA]. And Death has the key to the miser's chest [ASH], for The shroud has no pockets [EGY], so Death pays all the debts [ENG], indeed Death rights everything [MALT]. Conveniently, Dead men don't bite [ROM], and Dead men tell no tales [ENG] either, so Look upon death as going home [CHI], for Even the dead in their vaults enjoy company [MAD]. In the end, Death defies the doctor [SCO], for When it's your time [BRA], Death is the last doctor [SWE], and You only sleep really well in your coffin [IND]. Remember, We don't even get death for free; as it costs us our life [RUS].

CODES

AB AUS - Aboriginal Australian
AFG - Afghan
AFR - African
AFR AME - African American
ALB - Albanian
AME - American
ANG - Angolan
ARAB - Arabian
ARAP - Arapaho
ARM - Armenian
ASH - Ashanti (Ghana)
AZE - Azeri
BAL - Balinese
BAS - Basque
BER - Berber
BIB - Bible
BOS - Bosnian
BOT - Botswanian
BRA - Brazilian
BUL - Bulgarian
BURM - Burmese
BURU - Burundian
CAME - Cameroonian
CAMB - Cambodian
CHI - Chinese

CONG - Congolese
DAN - Danish
DUT - Dutch
EGY - Egyptian
ENG - English
ERI - Eritrean
EST - Estonian
ETH - Ethiopian
FAR - Faroese
FIN - Finnish
FLEM - Flemish
FRE - French
GEOR - Georgian
GER - German
GRE - Greek
GYP - Gypsy
HAW - Hawaiian
HEB - Hebrew
HUN - Hungarian
ICE - Icelandic
IND - Indian
INDO - Indonesian
INU - Inuit
IRI - Irish
ITA - Italian

IVO - Ivory Coast
JAM - Jamaican
JAP - Japanese
KASH - Kashmiri
KEN - Kenyan
KOR - Korean
KUR - Kurdish
KYR - Kyrgyz
LEB - Lebanese
MAD - Madagascan
MALAW - Malawian
MALAY - Malaysian
MALT - Maltese
MALI - Malian
MEX - Mexican
MON - Mongolian
NAM - Namibian
NAT AME - Native American
NEP - Nepali
NIG - Nigerian
NOR - Norwegian
PER - Persian
PHIL - Filipino
POL - Polish
POLY - Polynesian

POR - Portuguese
ROM - Roman
ROMA - Romanian
RUS - Russian
SAM - Samoan
SCO - Scottish
SLO - Slovenian
SPA - Spanish
SUD - Sudanese
SWA - Swahili
SWE - Swedish
TAM - Tamil
TAN - Tanzanian
TIB - Tibetan
THAI - Thai
TUR - Turkish
UGA - Ugandan
UKR - Ukrainian
UZB - Uzbek
VIET - Vietnamese
WEL - Welsh
YEM - Yemeni
ZEN - Zen Buddhist
ZIM - Zimbabwean
Others named in full

ILLUSTRATIONS

Cover: *The Hares and The Frogs* by Wenceslaus Hollar [1607-1677]
Frontispiece: *Sailing Boat*, by Hector McDonnell, 2014
Title Page: *Gipsies Fortune Telling*, Woodcut, Basle, 1552
Opposite Contents: *Dementia*, by Pieter van der Heyden [1530-1572]
Opposite page 1: *Pasiphaë*, by John Buckland Wright [1897-1954]
Page 4: *Children mocking Elisha*, by Hans Holbein the Younger, 1538
Page 7: *Arrival of the King*, 15th C. woodcut, from a book by Guido Delle Colonne [13th C.]
Page 9: *Reynard the Fox*, woodcut by Sebastian Münster [1488-1552]
Page 11: *The Decision of the Flowers*, by Henry Moses [1782-1870]
Page 13: *Tossing the Pancake*, by George Cruikshank [1792-1878]
Page 15: *Key to the heart*, 19th C, artist unknown
Page 17: *Battle*, 15th C. woodcut, from a book by Guido Delle Colonne [13th C.]
Page 19: *Haymaking*, medieval woodcut.
Page 21: *Michaelmas Day*, by George Cruikshank [1792-1878]
Page 22: *Dryads*, engraved by Pierre Milan, Paris, 16th C.
Page 25: *Golden Head by Golden Head*, by Dante Gabriel Rossetti [1828-1882]

Page 27: *Wedding Feast* by Wenceslaus Hollar [1607-1677]
Page 29: *Illustration from The Pickwick Papers* by Hablot Knight Brown [1815-1882]
Page 31: *Poliphilo & the Nymphs*, from *Hypnerotomachia*, Venice 1499
Page 33: *Sloth*, by Pieter Bruegel the Elder [1525-1569]
Page 35: *Greenwich Park*, by George Cruikshank [1792-1878]
Page 36: *A Midnight Modern Conversation*, by William Hogarth [1697-1764]
Page 39: *Goats eating leaves*, by Hector McDonnell, 2014
Page 41: *Hope*, by Pieter Bruegel the Elder [1525-1569]
Page 43: *War in Heaven*, 14th C. wood engraving
Page 45: *The Basilisk & the Weasel* by Wenceslaus Hollar [1607-1677]
Page 46: *Ladies in Parliament*, 1885, by George Cruikshank [1792-1878]
Page 49: *Big Fish Eat Little Fish*, by Pieter van der Heyden [1530-1572]
Page 51: *Avarice*, by Pieter van der Heyden [1530-1572] after Pieter Bruegel the Elder [1525-1569]
Page 53: *Fear and Hope are Vision*, by William Blake [1757-1827]
Page 54: *Adam and Eve*, by Pierre Lombart, 1660
Page 57: *The Dancing Deaths*, from Schedel's *Liber Chronicarum*, 1493.